PIANO · VOCAL · GUITAR

MOTOWN 45th

ANNIVERSARY SONGBOOK

ISBN 0-634-08634-0

HAL·LEONARD®
CORPORATION
7777 W. BLUEMOUND RD. P.O. BOX 13819 MILWAUKEE, WI 53213

Visit Hal Leonard Online at
www.halleonard.com

4	AIN'T NO MOUNTAIN HIGH ENOUGH
10	ALL NIGHT LONG (ALL NIGHT)
20	BABY I NEED YOUR LOVIN'
17	BABY LOVE
26	DO YOU LOVE ME
32	ENDLESS LOVE
38	GET READY
41	I CAN'T HELP MYSELF (SUGAR PIE, HONEY BUNCH)
46	I HEARD IT THROUGH THE GRAPEVINE
50	I SECOND THAT EMOTION
54	I WISH
59	I'LL BE THERE
64	IT TAKES TWO
67	JUST TO SEE HER
74	LET'S GET IT ON
81	MY GIRL
88	NEITHER ONE OF US (WANTS TO BE THE FIRST TO SAY GOODBYE)
94	NIGHTSHIFT
104	REACH OUT AND TOUCH (SOMEBODY'S HAND)
108	SIGNED, SEALED, DELIVERED I'M YOURS
99	STANDING IN THE SHADOWS OF LOVE
112	STOP! IN THE NAME OF LOVE
117	SUPERSTITION
122	THE WAY YOU DO THE THINGS YOU DO
124	WHAT BECOMES OF THE BROKEN HEARTED
128	WHAT'S GOING ON
134	YOU CAN'T HURRY LOVE
138	YOU KEEP ME HANGIN' ON

AIN'T NO MOUNTAIN HIGH ENOUGH

Words and Music by NICKOLAS ASHFORD
and VALERIE SIMPSON

With a steady beat

Now, if you need me, call ____ me. No mat-ter where you
I set you free? _____ I told you you could

are, no mat-ter ____ how ____ far. Don't wor-ry, ba - by. Just call out ____ my name.
al - ways count on ____ me. ____ And from that day ____ on, ____ I made __ a vow:

____ I'll be there in a hur - ry. ____ You don't have to wor - ry, 'cause ba - by there
____ I'll be there when you want ____ me, ____ some way ____ some - how. ____ 'Cause ba - by there

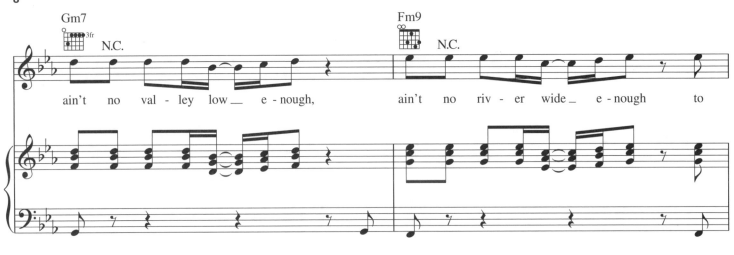

ain't no val-ley low __ e-nough, ain't no riv-er wide __ e-nough to

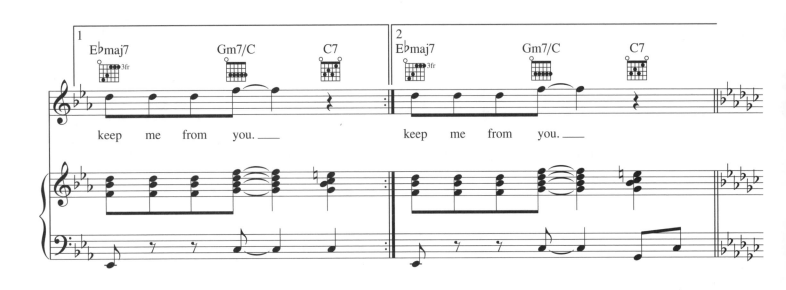

keep me from you. _____ keep me from you. _____

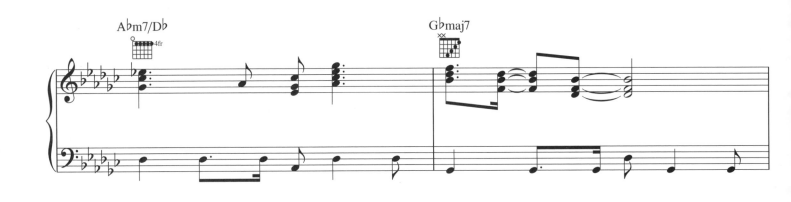

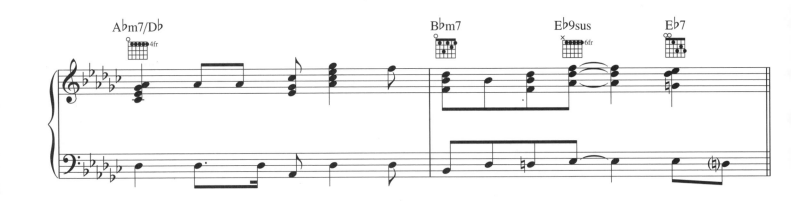

ALL NIGHT LONG
(All Night)

Words and Music by
LIONEL RICHIE

12

BABY LOVE

Words and Music by BRIAN HOLLAND,
EDWARD HOLLAND and LAMONT DOZIER

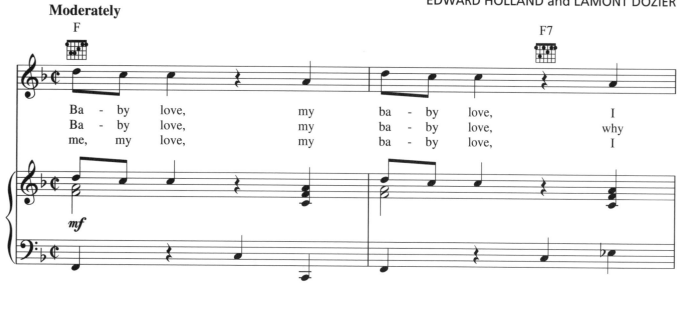

Ba - by love, my ba - by love, I
Ba - by love, my ba - by love, why
me, my love, my ba - by love, I

need you oh how I need ___ you. But all you do is
must we sep - a - rate my love? All of my
need ya, oh how I need ___ ya. Why you do me

treat me bad, _____ break my heart and leave me sad. _____
whole life through, _____ I nev - er love no one but you. _____
like you do, _____ af - ter I've been true to you? _____

BABY I NEED YOUR LOVIN'

Words and Music by BRIAN HOLLAND,
LAMONT DOZIER and EDWARD HOLLAND

DO YOU LOVE ME

Words and Music by
BERRY GORDY

ENDLESS LOVE

Words and Music by
LIONEL RICHIE

Oh, _____ and __ love, _____

GET READY

Words and Music by
WILLIAM "SMOKEY" ROBINSON

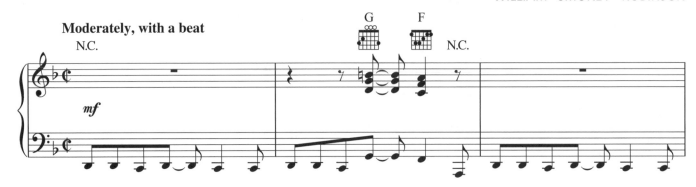

Moderately, with a beat

I

nev- er met a girl who makes ___ me feel ___ the way that
wan - na play ___ hide and seek ___ with love, ___ let me re-
All ___ my ___ friends should - n't want me to, ___ I un - der-

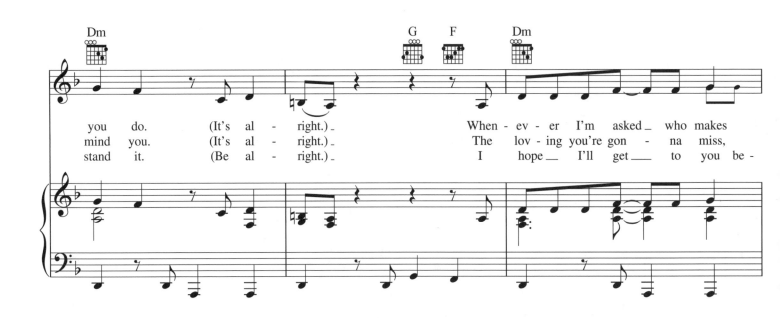

you do. (It's al - right.) ___
mind you. (It's al - right.) ___
stand it. (Be al - right.) ___

When - ev - er I'm asked ___ who makes
The lov - ing you're gon - na miss,
I hope ___ I'll get ___ to you be-

I CAN'T HELP MYSELF
(Sugar Pie, Honey Bunch)

Words and Music by BRIAN HOLLAND,
LAMONT DOZIER and EDWARD HOLLAND

Moderately fast

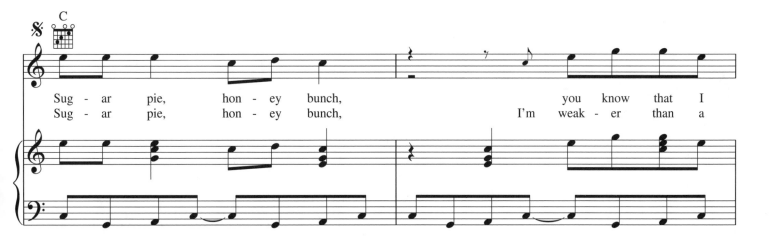

Sug- ar pie, hon- ey bunch, you know that I
Sug- ar pie, hon- ey bunch, I'm weak- er than a

love you. ___ I can't help my- self,
man should be. I can't help my- self,

I HEARD IT
THROUGH THE GRAPEVINE

Words and Music by NORMAN J. WHITFIELD
and BARRETT STRONG

Lyrics:

Mm._____ I bet you're won-derin' how I knew
_____ ain't sup-posed to cry,
_____ of what you see,

'bout your plans _____ to make me blue, _____ with some oth-er guy
but these tears _____ I can't hold in-side. _____ Los-in' you _____
son, and none _____ of what you hear. _____ But I can't help _____

D.S. al Coda

Peo - ple say be - lieve half ___

CODA

___ yeah, yeah, ___ yeah. I heard it through the grape - vine, not much

Repeat and Fade

long - er would you be mine, ba - by. Yeah, ___

I SECOND THAT EMOTION

Words and Music by WILLIAM "SMOKEY" ROBINSON
and ALFRED CLEVELAND

I WISH

Words and Music by
STEVIE WONDER

Bright Funk

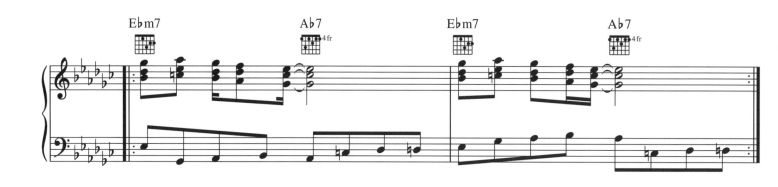

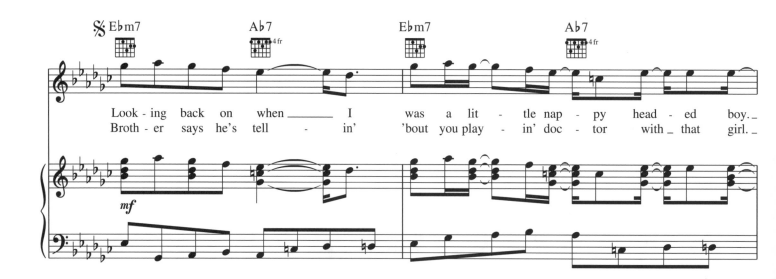

Look - ing back on when _____ I was a lit - tle nap - py head - ed boy. __
Broth - er says he's tell - in' 'bout you play - in' doc - tor with __ that girl. __

days ev - er have to go, 'cause I loved them so. __ Do do __ do do __ do

do do do do do do do, __ do do __ do do __ do do do do do do. __

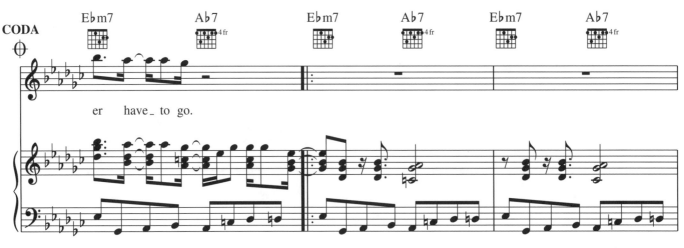

er have to go.

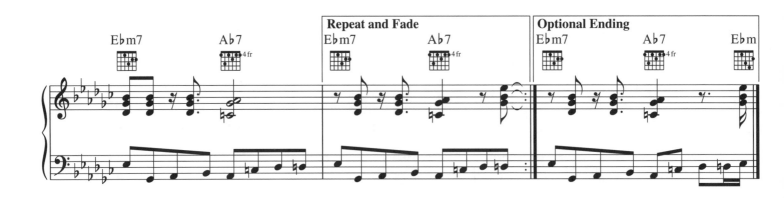

I'LL BE THERE

Words and Music by BERRY GORDY,
HAL DAVIS, WILLIE HUTCH and BOB WEST

IT TAKES TWO

Words and Music by WILLIAM STEVENSON
and SYLVIA MOY

Fast Rock

1. One can have a dream, __ ba - by, __ Two can make that dream __ so __
2., 3. *(See additional lyrics)*

__ real. __ One can talk a - bout be - ing in love, __ Two can

say how it real - ly feels. __ One can wish up - on

Additional Lyrics

2. One can have a broken heart, living in misery,
   Two can really ease the pain like the perfect remedy.
   One can be alone in a crowd, like an island he's all alone,
   Two can make it just-a any place seem just like being home.
   Chorus

3. One can go out to a movie, looking for a special treat,
   Two can make that a single movie something really kind-a sweet,
   One can take a walk in the moonlight, thinking that it's really nice,
   Ah but two walking a-hand in hand is like adding just a pinch of spice.
   Chorus

JUST TO SEE HER

Words and Music by JIMMY GEORGE
and LOU PARDINI

LET'S GET IT ON

Words and Music by MARVIN GAYE
and ED TOWNSEND

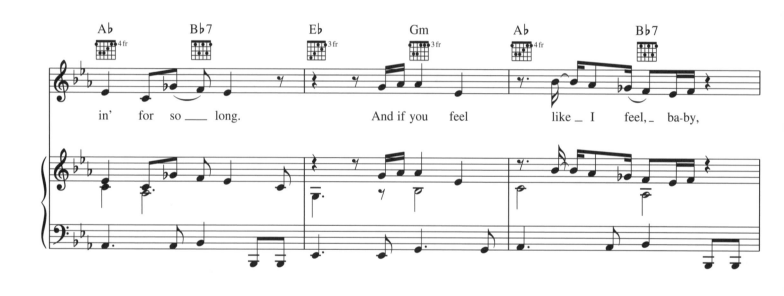

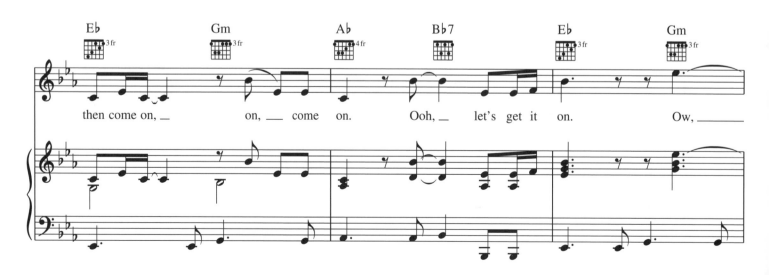

MY GIRL

Words and Music by WILLIAM "SMOKEY" ROBINSON
and RONALD WHITE

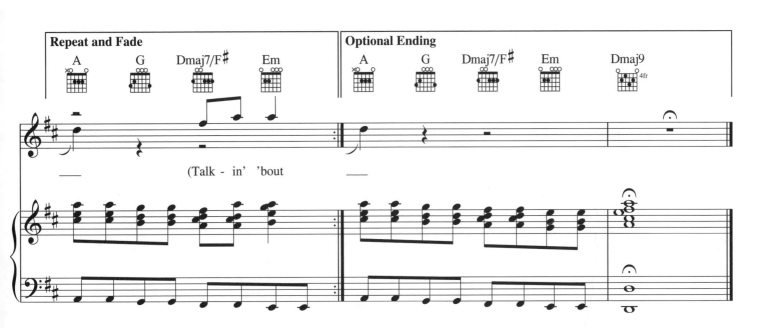

NEITHER ONE OF US
(Wants to Be the First to Say Goodbye)

Words and Music by
JIM WEATHERLY

NIGHTSHIFT

Words and Music by WALTER ORANGE,
DENNIS LAMBERT and FRANNE GOLDE

Am7

Am7/D

you can ___ see ___ what's go - in' on. ___
we'll be ___ there ___ at your ___ side. ___

Em

Say you will ___

Am7

Cmaj9

sing your ___ songs ___ for - ev - er - more ___ (ev - er - more).

G

Em

C

Gon - na be some sweet sounds ___ com - in' down ___ on the

STANDING IN THE SHADOWS OF LOVE

Words and Music by EDWARD HOLLAND,
LAMONT DOZIER and BRIAN HOLLAND

Stand-ing in the shad-ows of love, _____ I'm get-ting
Stand-ing in the shad-ows of love, _____ I'm get-ting

read-y for the heart-aches to come. _____ Can't you see me
read-y for the heart-aches to come. _____ Don't you see me

stand-ing in the shad-ows of love? _____ I'm get-ting
stand-ing in the shad-ows of love? _____ Try my best _ to get

REACH OUT AND TOUCH
(Somebody's Hand)

Words and Music by NICKOLAS ASHFORD
and VALERIE SIMPSON

SIGNED, SEALED, DELIVERED I'M YOURS

Words and Music by STEVIE WONDER,
SYREETA WRIGHT, LEE GARRETT and LULA MAE HARDAWAY

Moderately

Like a fool I went and stayed __ too long. __
Then that time I went and said __ good - bye. __
Seen a lot of things in this __ old world. _
Ooh - wee babe, you set my world __ on fire. __

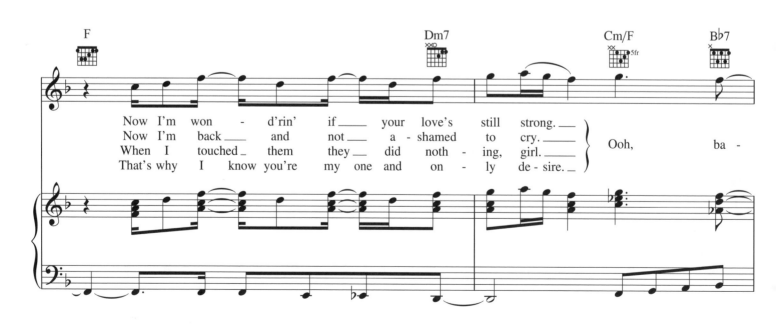

Now I'm won - d'rin' if __ your love's still strong. __
Now I'm back __ and not __ a - shamed to cry. __
When I touched __ them they __ did noth - ing, girl. __
That's why I know you're my one and on - ly de - sire. __

Ooh, ba -

STOP! IN THE NAME OF LOVE

Words and Music by LAMONT DOZIER,
BRIAN HOLLAND and EDWARD HOLLAND

Steadily

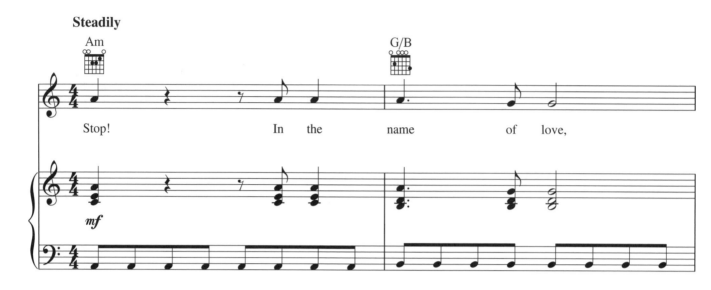

Stop! In the name of love,

be - fore you break my heart.

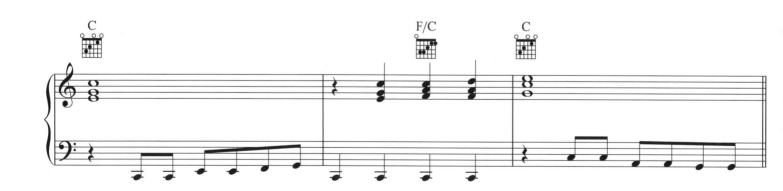

SUPERSTITION

Words and Music by
STEVIE WONDER

- tious, ____
- lems. ____
- tious. ____

lad - der's 'bout __ to fall. ____
Do all that __ you can.
The dev - il's on __ his way. ____

—

(1., 3.) Thir - teen month _ old ba -
(2.) Keep me in ____ a day -

- by ____
- dream. _

broke _ the look - ing glass.
Keep _ me go - in' strong.

Sev - en years _ of bad _
You don't wan - na save _

Ooh, __ ver - y su - per - sti -

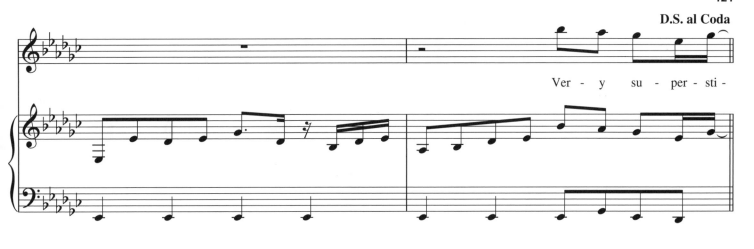

D.S. al Coda

Ver - y su - per - sti -

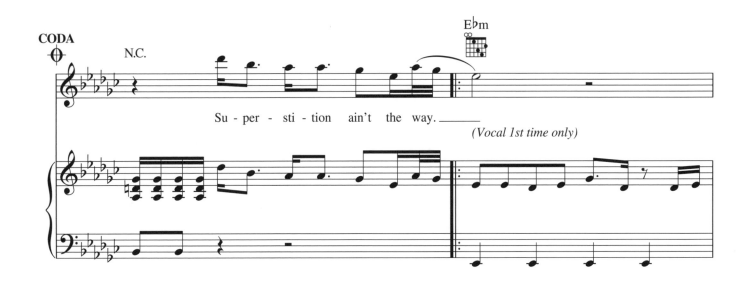

CODA

N.C.

E♭m

Su - per - sti -tion ain't the way. _____

(Vocal 1st time only)

Repeat and Fade

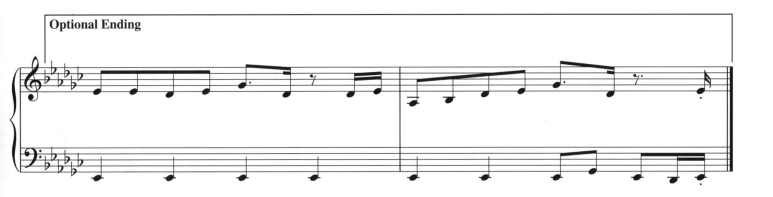

Optional Ending

THE WAY YOU DO THE THINGS YOU DO

Words and Music by WILLIAM "SMOKEY" ROBINSON
and ROBERT ROGERS

WHAT BECOMES OF THE BROKEN HEARTED

Words and Music by JAMES A. DEAN,
PAUL RISER and WILLIAM HENRY WEATHERSPOON

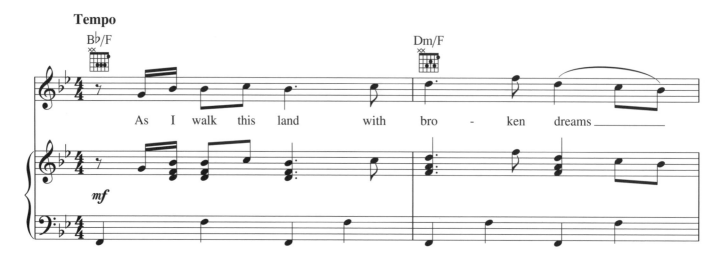

As I walk this land with bro-ken dreams ____

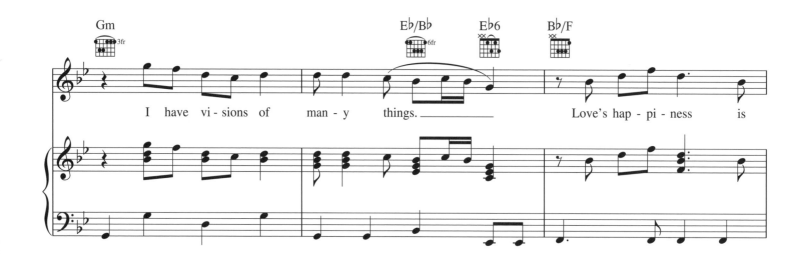

I have vi-sions of man-y things. ____ Love's hap-pi-ness is

just an il-lu-sion filled with sad-ness ____ and con-fu-sion. ____

WHAT'S GOING ON

Words and Music by MARVIN GAYE,
AL CLEVELAND and RENALDO BENSON

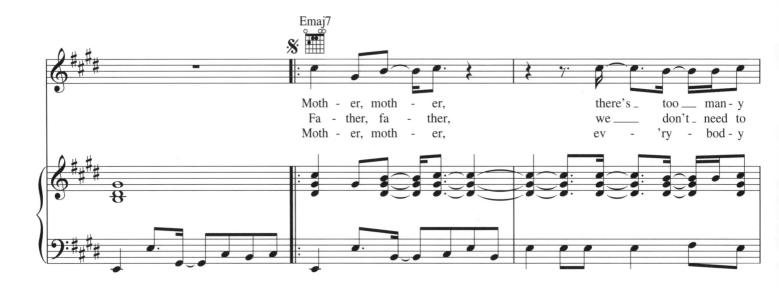

Moth - er, moth - er,   there's __ too __ man - y
Fa - ther, fa - ther,   we _____ don't _ need to
Moth - er, moth - er,   ev - 'ry - bod - y

of you cry - ing.
es - ca - late. _____
thinks we're wrong. ___

Broth - er, broth - er, broth - er,
You see, _ war is not __ the an - swer,
Ah, but __ who are they _ to judge _ us

ya, ya, ya.

I, yi, yi, yi, yi, yi, ya, ya, ya, ya, ya.

A/B

Be, doot, de, doot; Be, be, be, doot; Be be, be, doot;

Repeat and Fade

Bu, doot, be, be, be, doot; Be, be, be, be, be, doot. Ooh,

YOU CAN'T HURRY LOVE

Words and Music by EDWARD HOLLAND,
LAMONT DOZIER and BRIAN HOLLAND

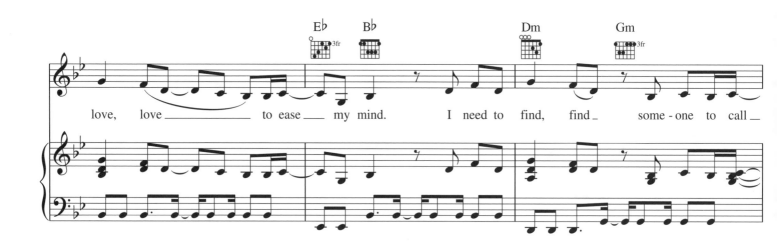

YOU KEEP ME HANGIN' ON

Words and Music by EDWARD HOLLAND,
LAMONT DOZIER and BRIAN HOLLAND

Recorded a half step lower.

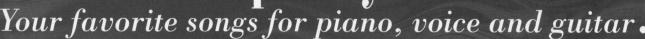

Contemporary Classics

Your favorite songs for piano, voice and guitar.

The Definitive Rock 'n' Roll Collection

A classic collection of the best songs from the early rock 'n' roll years – 1955-1966. 97 songs, including: Barbara Ann • Chantilly Lace • Dream Lover • Duke of Earl • Earth Angel • Great Balls of Fire • Louie, Louie • Rock Around the Clock • Ruby Baby • Runaway • (Seven Little Girls) Sitting in the Back Seat • Stay • Surfin' U.S.A. • Wild Thing • Woolly Bully • and more.

00490195 ....$29.95

The Big Book of Rock

78 of rock's biggest hits, including: Addicted to Love • American Pie • Born to Be Wild • Cold As Ice • Dust in the Wind • Free Bird • Goodbye Yellow Brick Road • Groovin' • Hey Jude • I Love Rock 'N' Roll • Lay Down Sally • Layla • Livin' on a Prayer • Louie Louie • Maggie May • Me and Bobby McGee • Monday, Monday • Owner of a Lonely Heart • Shout • Walk This Way • We Didn't Start the Fire • You Really Got Me • and more.

00311566..$19.95

Big Book of Movie Music

Features 73 classic songs from 72 movies: Beauty and the Beast • Change the World • Eye of the Tiger • I Finally Found Someone • The John Dunbar Theme • Somewhere in Time • Stayin' Alive • Take My Breath Away • Unchained Melody • The Way You Look Tonight • You've Got a Friend in Me • Zorro's Theme • more.

00311582 ....$19.95

The Best Rock Songs Ever

70 of the best rock songs from yesterday and today, including: All Day and All of the Night • All Shook Up • Blue Suede Shoes • Born to Be Wild • Boys Are Back in Town • Every Breath You Take • Faith • Free Bird • Hey Jude • I Still Haven't Found What I'm Looking For • Livin' on a Prayer • Lola • Louie Louie • Maggie May • Money • (She's) Some Kind of Wonderful • Takin' Care of Business • Walk This Way • We Didn't Start the Fire • We Got the Beat • Wild Thing • more!

00490424 ....$18.95

Contemporary Vocal Groups

This exciting new collection includes 35 huge hits by 18 of today's best vocal groups, including 98 Degrees, TLC, Destiny's Child, Savage Garden, Boyz II Men, Dixie Chicks, 'N Sync, and more! Songs include: Bills, Bills, Bills • Bug a Boo • Diggin' on You • The Hardest Thing • I'll Make Love to You • In the Still of the Nite (I'll Remember) • Ready to Run • Tearin' Up My Heart • Truly, Madly, Deeply • Waterfalls • Wide Open Spaces • and more.

00310605 ....$14.95

Motown Anthology

This songbook commemorates Motown's 40th Anniversary with 68 songs, background information on this famous record label, and lots of photos. Songs include: ABC • Baby Love • Ben • Dancing in the Street • Easy • For Once in My Life • My Girl • Shop Around • The Tracks of My Tears • War • What's Going On • You Can't Hurry Love • and many more.

00310367 ....$19.95

Best Contemporary Ballads

Includes 35 favorites: And So It Goes • Angel • Beautiful in My Eyes • Don't Know Much • Fields of Gold • Hero • I Will Remember You • Iris • My Heart Will Go On • Tears in Heaven • Valentine • You Were Meant for Me • You'll Be in My Heart • and more.

00310583 ....$16.95

Contemporary Hits

Contains 35 favorites by artists such as Sarah McLachlan, Whitney Houston, 'N Sync, Mariah Carey, Christina Aguilera, Celine Dion, and other top stars. Songs include: Adia • Building a Mystery • The Hardest Thing • I Believe in You and Me • I Drive Myself Crazy • I'll Be • Kiss Me • My Father's Eyes • Reflection • Smooth • Torn • and more!

00310589..$16.95

Jock Rock Hits

32 stadium-shaking favorites, including: Another One Bites the Dust • The Boys Are Back in Town • Freeze-Frame • Gonna Make You Sweat (Everybody Dance Now) • I Got You (I Feel Good) • Na Na Hey Hey Kiss Him Goodbye • Rock & Roll – Part II (The Hey Song) • Shout • Tequila • We Are the Champions • We Will Rock You • Whoomp! (There It Is) • Wild Thing • and more.

00310105...$14.95

Rock Ballads

31 sentimental favorites, including: All for Love • Bed of Roses • Dust in the Wind • Everybody Hurts • Right Here Waiting • Tears in Heaven • and more.

00311673...$14.95

0402